THE

WOMAN

I KEPT

TO

MYSELF

THE WOMAN I KEPT TO MYSELF

poems

by Julia Alvarez

Algonquin Books
of Chapel Hill
2004

Published by

ALGONQUIN BOOKS OF CHAPEL HILL

Post Office Box 2225

Chapel Hill, North Carolina 27515-2225

a division of

Workman Publishing

708 Broadway

New York, New York 10003

Library of Congress Cataloging-in-Publication Data

Alvarez, Julia.

    The woman I kept to myself : poems /

  by Julia Alvarez.— 1st ed.

     p. cm.

   ISBN 1-56512-406-5

   1. Women—Poetry.   I. Title.

PS3551.L845W66 2004

811'.54—dc22   2003070807

10 9 8 7 6 5 4 3 2 1

First Edition

for
Judy

para
Tití

To whom do we tell what happened on the earth?

—Czeslaw Milosz

CONTENTS

Keeping Watch

THE

WOMAN

I KEPT

TO

MYSELF

Seven Trees

FAMILY TREE

When I was born, my mother wrote me down
on the family tree, a second bough
dangling from her branch which was attached
to a great trunk which sunk down into roots
sprung from the seeds of Spain and Africa,
the latter never mentioned but expressed
by darker faces in the family clan.
We were on the up and up, "good" hair, light skin,
a foreign education for the men,
fine weddings for the guaranteed virgins.

Branch by branch, blossom by blossom, we grew:
our individual trees lost in the woods
of Alvarez and Tavares ancestors.
Until by emigration, seeds were cast
on foreign lands: a maternal great-aunt
married a German and our name was lost
in guttural patronymics, blond cousins
with year-round suntans. My sisters and I,
transported stateside in the sixties, turned
into tangle-haired hippies, slinging our English slang.

We clipped ourselves off from the family tree,
independent women! Or so we thought,
until our babies started to be born,
sporting Mamita's dimples, Tío's brows,
the voice of Tía Mariana, thick and sweet
like boiled-down sugarcane: the family tree
transplanted but not totally transformed.
Even I, the childless one, intend to write
New Yorker fiction in the Cheever style,
but all my stories tell where I came from.

SAMÁN

Ciudad Trujillo, 1957

The samán tree grew on our property
near where we bordered an abandoned lot,
fenced off with barbed wire, a no-man's-land
we children were forbidden to explore.
Especially after the squatters came,
poor campesinos with their eyesore shacks,
hidden by double hedgerows from our house.
But from the branches of that tall samán,
we could see their tin roofs, their cooking fires,
their naked kids, their clotheslines hung with rags.

Beyond them stretched the military strip
where El Jefe's elite and airborne corps
practiced maneuvers, roaring toward the sky,
their steel sides glinting, wings flashing like knives,
as if to clear a pathway up to God
and bring back all those disappeared below.
Waving, we watched them as they plummeted,
tanks rushing toward them in reconnaissance,
gun blasts shaking the branches where we sat.
It was our perch into the heart of darkness.

One day, the last day of my childhood,
as we straddled a branch, my sister told
the bloody politics of the body:
how I would bleed, how babies came to be,
how I would labor in delivery.
Then she swore me to secrecy or else
something so horrible she couldn't tell
would happen! "*Or else* what?" I begged to know.
But she climbed down and left me looking at
what had already happened to the world.

WEEPING WILLOW

New York, 1960–1961

The first time I saw my father crying
we were already living in New York
in a dark sublet on a second floor,
from which we could see nothing but concrete—
stone buildings, a cold and marbled sky—
more like the landscape of a prison yard
with pale jailors speaking gibberish
than the dictatorship we had escaped.
Amid the noise of traffic and English,
it was a silent world—till Papi cried.

He bent over his chair, holding his sides,
while Mami rushed around, shutting windows,
afraid the Super would warn us again
about the level of our noise, the smell
of garlic wafting through our vents.
We had been looking for another place,
maybe out in the suburbs with some trees,
where we might feel at ease being ourselves.
When Mami hushed him, Papi wiped his face,
burying his grief inside his handkerchief.

A year later, we rented a small house
with its own yard in which there grew a tree
I'd never seen before: its long branches
hung down and wept when the wind blew through them.
One winter night my father woke us up
to our first blizzard. At the bay window,
we watched the backyard slowly fill with snow—
the bushes, lawn chairs, swing set, garbage pails,
the branches of the willow disappeared,
and one by one we all burst into tears.

MAPLE, OAK, OR ELM?

Syracuse, 1973–1975

Maple or oak or elm? By now I know
how to tell them apart. Yet when I think
of falling in love as a young woman
I think of my confusion naming them —
maple, oak, elm? One of them always grew
outside the bedroom window where I lay
waiting for passion to wash over me.
What did I know of love but that I gave
my body for the chance to play
the happy heroine of a love story?

But I wasn't happy, I was lonely,
already knowing this was the wrong love
or rather the wrong life-story for me.
So I lay there, studying the tops of trees,
the map of branches that might orient me
as to where I was going by myself
after this heartbreak. With my eye, I traced
the traffic of the branches as they climbed
toward their destination in the sky,
losing myself in their hectic movements.

Until his love cry brought me back to earth,
down through the branches, the open window,
stealing like light across the bedroom floor,
over the rumpled sheets to this woman
who was and wasn't me, who didn't know
where she was going or whom she might be:
maybe the burning maple showing off,
or mighty oak synonymous with strength,
or vague elm whose unmistakable shape
can only be discerned from a distance.

ARBORVITAE

Champaign, 1985–1987

After the divorce, I moved to the heartland,
and the worst period of my life began:
sadness is too mild a word for the grief
I went through, and grief too noble-sounding
for the dull hopelessness I'll call despair
for lack of a better word. What else was left?
Life's guardrails were gone: I had no kids
to keep me this side of the edge, no man
asking where had I put his dressy shoes,
no golden lab wagging its welcome tail

as I entered the one-room bungalow
whose owners, a young couple, lived next door,
proving the love story I had failed at.
Separating my rental from their house
was a hedge with a fancy Latin name,
arborvitae, pruned by the husband,
who came outside on weekends to maintain
Its Comeliness, the title I gave it,
mocking its tactful function as a screen
to keep me out of sight of the owners.

When they divorced, I searched for a new place
with room for a writing room. I unpacked
the poems I had abandoned in a box
and got to work. From the study window
I looked out at an almost treeless view —
the Midwest ravaged by Dutch elm disease —
but for a ragged windbreak of scarred trees,
which turned out to be arborvitae, too.
But now these *trees of life* seemed rightly named,
buffeted by the hard winds of the heartland.

LOCUST

Weybridge, 1998

Happiness surprised me in middle age:
just in the nick of forty I found love,
a steady job, a publisher, a home,
ten acres and a sky-reflecting pond—
a better ending than I'd expected.
We built our own house on a bare hillside
and started planting trees: elm, maple, oak.
Under my second-story writing room
(which was all windows on the southeast side)
we put in locusts for their "instant shade."

By our third anniversary those trees
were grown so tall, it was like climbing up
into a tree house when I went to work,
pulling the mind's ladder up behind me
from the absorbing life I was living.
I tried to focus but those branches filled
with songbirds busy at their nest building,
squirrels scampering to the very edges
of blossoming branches buzzing with bees.
How could I write with all this activity?

It took some getting used to but, of course,
life feeds life. Where'd I get the idea
that art and happiness could never jive?
I felt stupid, wasting so many years.
But I took solace from those locust trees,
known for their crooked, seemingly aimless growth.
We have to live our natures out, the seed
we call our soul unfolds over the course
of a lifetime and there's no going back
on who we are—that much I've learned from trees.

LAST TREES

When I think of my death, I think of trees
in the full of summer, a row of them
marking a border, still too far away
for me to name them, posted with rotted boards
everyone but the faint of heart ignores.
(By then, I hope not to be one of those.)
I want to go boldly to the extreme
edge of a life I've lived to the fullest
and climb over the tumbled rocks or crawl
under the wire, never looking back—

for if I were to turn and see the house
perched on its hillside, windows flashing light,
or hear a dear voice calling from the deck,
"Supper's on the table!" I might lose heart,
and turn back from those trees, telling myself,
tomorrow is a better day to die.
I'd race to beat the darkness to the door,
thrashing and stumbling through the underbrush,
flushing out red-winged blackbirds, shaking loose
seeds for next summer's weeds from their packed pods—

only to look up, breathless, and realize
the hillside's gone, I'm surrounded by trees
that I don't recognize, Dante's dark wood
closing in on all sides, my last moments
filled with a fear that takes my breath away.
Better not to look back until I've reached
that line of trees I've used to mark my life,
naming them as I pass under their boughs
into the growing shadows: *maple, willow,*
oak, arborvitae, locust, elm, samán.

The Woman I Kept to Myself

INTIMATIONS OF MORTALITY FROM A RECOLLECTION IN EARLY CHILDHOOD

Looking down at my arm
I see the roundness taut around the bone,
the smooth youth of the skin, the tiny pores,
the hair as if not my own, fine hairs bleached by the sun,
the freckling constellations (a wing, a fan?),
the tiny sparklings of perspiration,
a glow as if someone has taken a rag
to a clouded surface and rubbed hard—
and, aha! see there! (I am seven years old!)
a face begins to form.

Oh, lovely arm, I have never seen before
at the end of my shoulder, whence did you come from?
Travel with me through life with your mate to match.
How will I bear to see you braceleted,
strapped with a watch, holding a newborn son?
But how can I stop this grand progression?
The clocks are ticking in the cricket grass,
a voice is calling from the far-off house,
the night is falling, the stars go round and round,
I taste the rotting leaves, the burning sun.

I put my arm up to my face and smell
as a dog is given a lost child's dress to smell.
I am already lost, beyond repair —
the tiny pores, fine hair, the alarming arm!
The voice grows urgent: *Time to come in!*
Time to eat! Time to get out of the sun!
(Of course, my life would have to catch up with me.)
But ah, the heady, sweaty arm, tasting of tears —
I lift it high, turn it this way and that,
It is mine, my prize, a body that's going to die!

ANGER & ART

As a child, I hated statues, comic books.
I sighed whenever I was given a doll—
these stand-ins for living beings angered me.
Stuffed animals on my bed drove me to tears.
Why settle for Snoopy, Barbie, baby dolls?
I wanted a puppy, slurping on my face;
a teenage friend with a boyfriend and real breasts;
a baby who'd do more than close her eyes
when I laid her down! Where did this rage
against the mockery of art come from?

What did I know? I was only a child
with my immortal life ahead of me.
Nothing I loved was dying. (What was death?
Somebody's costume at a masquerade?
I hated masquerades!) But time was ticking:
a baby cousin in a puffy box;
my teacher's science bulletins at school:
The sunlight on your face is eight years old.
The twinkling stars you wish on have gone out.
How could I bear a world where nothing held?

Everything, everything falling through the sieve
into the graveyard of the past: puppies,
babies, teenagers, mothers, fathers, *me*—
all of us swirling round in that whirl of time!
This was a rough epiphany for a kid
with a passion for the real. I held my breath,
hoping to make it stop—until I blacked out—
and woke up to a dying world, old sunlight
shining on my face, a child no more,
now that I knew what art and rage were for.

EL FOTÓGRAFO

Each time he came with his black hood and box
to record a special day, a baby's birth,
a first communion, someone taking off
to Nueva York, a divorced aunt's return
from a trip to France, an advanced degree
by the family intellectual,
or the announcement of religious vows
by the plain cousin (*pobrecita!*)
with the faint mustache and the heart of gold—
a gathering of the tribe, two dozen strong,

scrubbed, perfumed, permed, coifed, and gussied up,
a command performance at my grandparents' house,
while he, dressed cheaply in a faded suit,
sweat beading his brow, struggled to record
that unforgettable day, posing us
in perfect order, faces to the sun,
jokes cracked for smiles, cowlicks patted down,
sashes and bows retied, the boys' flies checked:
a perfect tableau for posterity,
hereditary gods and goddesses—

but every time he was about to snap,
a giggling bout attacked the children's row
or Tío sneezed or Abuelita burped
or someone who wouldn't fess up farted,
and the portrait was ruined! He'd poke out
his mournful face from under his black hood,
glancing around at his marred masterpiece,
his passion trivialized, his art abused—
pobrecito! Now I know how he felt
struggling to get all that life on paper.

THE RED PICKUP

The wish I always made in childhood
before the blazing candles or when asked
what gift I wanted the Three Kings to bring
was a red pickup, which Mami vetoed
as inappropriate. And so I improvised,
trading in speed for a pair of cowboy boots,
bright red with rawhide tassels that would swing
when I swaggered into my fourth-grade class
asking for an exemption from homework
from my strict teacher, Mrs. Brown from Maine.

She called my mother weekly to complain
of my misbehaviors, among them
a tendency to daydream instead of
finding the common denominator.
(But what had I in common with fractions?
I wanted the bigger, undivided world!)
She was one more woman in a series
of dissuaders against that red pickup
in all its transformations, which at root
was a driving desire to be a part

of something bigger than a pretty girl,
the wild, exciting world reserved for boys:
guns that shot noisy *hellos!* in the air
and left crimson roses on clean, white shirts;
firecrackers with scarlet explosions
that made even my deaf grandfather jump.
I wanted what God wanted when He made
the world, to be a driving force, a creator.
And that red pickup was my only ride
out of the common denominator.

SPIC

U.S.A., 1960

Out in the playground, kids were shouting *Spic!*
lifting my sister's skirt, yanking her slip.
Younger, less sexy, I was held and stripped
of coat and bookbag. Homework tumbled out
into oncoming traffic on the street.
Irregular verbs crumpled under tires
of frantic taxis, blew against the grates
of uptown buses we would later take
when school let out, trailed by cries of *Spic!*
What did they want, these American kids?

That night when we asked Mami, she explained:
our classmates had been asking us to *speak*,
not to be so unfriendly, running off
without a word. "This is América!
The anthem here invites its citizens
to speak up. *Oh see, can you say,*" she sang,
proving her point, making us sing along.
She winked at Papi, who had not joined in
but bowed his head, speaking instead to God
to protect his daughters in America.

I took her at her word: I raised my hand,
speaking up during classes, recess time.
The boys got meaner. *Spic ball!* they called out,
tossing off my school beanie, playing catch
while I ran boy to boy to get it back.
They sacked my stolen lunch box for their snacks,
dumping the foreign things in the garbage bin,
Spic trash! But I kept talking, telling them
how someday when I'd learn their language well,
I'd say what I'd seen in America.

ALL-AMERICAN GIRL

I wanted stockings, makeup, store-bought clothes;
I wanted to look like an American girl;
to speak my English so you couldn't tell
I'd come from somewhere else. I locked myself
in the bathroom, trying to match my face
with words in my new language: *grimace, leer,
disgust, disdain*—feelings I had yet to feel
in English. (And would *tristeza* even feel
the same as *sadness* with its Saxon sound?
Would *pity* look as soulful as *piedad*?)

I didn't know if I could ever show
genuine feeling in a borrowed tongue.
If *cortesía* would be misunderstood
as brown-nosing or cries of *alegría*
translate as terror. So, mirror in hand,
I practiced foreign faces, Anglo grins,
repressing a native Latin fluency
for the cooler mask of English ironies.
I wanted the world and words to match again
as when I had lived solely in Spanish.

But my face wouldn't obey—like a tide
it was pulled back by my lunatic heart
to its old habits of showing feelings.
Long after I'd lost my heavy accent,
my face showed I had come from somewhere else.
I couldn't keep the southern continent
out of the northern *vista* of my eyes,
or cut my *cara* off to spite my face.
I couldn't look like anybody else
but who I was: an all-American girl.

BELLEVUE

My mother used to say that she'd end up
at Bellevue if we didn't all behave.
In the old country when we disobeyed,
she'd drop us off at the cloistered Carmelites
and ring the bell and drive away. We sobbed
until the little lay nun led us in
to where a waiting sister, whose veiled face
we never saw, spoke to us through a grate
about the fourth commandment, telling us
how Jesus obeyed His mother and He was God.

In New York, Mami changed her tack and used
the threat of a mental breakdown to control
four runaway tempers, four strong-willed girls,
four of her own unruly selves who grew
unrulier in this land of the free.
I still remember how she would pretend
to call admissions, pack her suitcase up
with nothing but a toothbrush, showercap.
"I'm going to Bellevue, do what you want!"
She'd bang the front door, rush out to the car.

Who knows where she went on her hour off?
She needed to get away from her crazy girls,
who wanted lives she had raised them not to want.
So many tempting things in this new world,
so many young girls on their own, so many boys
with hands where hands did not belong.
Of course, she wanted to go to Bellevue,
where the world was safe, the grates familiar,
the howling not unlike her stifled sobs
as she drove around and around our block.

ABBOT ACADEMY

Mami sent me to Abbot where they tamed
wild girls—or so she'd heard—into ladies,
who knew to hold their skirts down in a breeze
and say "Excuse me" if compelled to speak;
ladies who married well, had lovely kids,
then inexplicably went mad and had
gin and tonics or the gardener for breakfast—
that part my mother hadn't heard; ladies
who learned to act like blondes even if they
were dark-haired, olive-skinned, spic-chicks like me.

And so that fall, with everything checked off
the master list—3 tea dresses, 2 pairs
of brown oxfords, white gloves, 4 cardigans—
I was deposited at Draper Hall
to have my edges rounded off, my roots
repotted in American soil.
I bit my nails, cracked my knuckles hard,
habits the handbook termed unladylike—
(*sins,* the nuns called them back at Catholic school).
I said my first prayer in months that night.

"Ay Dios," I begged, "help me survive this place."
And for the first time in America,
He listened: the next day for English class
I was assigned to Miss Ruth Stevenson
who closed the classroom door and said, "Ladies,
let's have ourselves a hell of a good time!"
And we did, reading Austen, Dickinson,
Eliot, Woolf, until we understood
we'd come to train — not tame — the wild girls
into the women who would run the world.

BY ACCIDENT

Sometimes I think I became the woman
I am by accident, nothing prepared
the way, not a dramatic, wayward aunt,
or moody mother who read *Middlemarch,*
or godmother who whispered, "You can be
whatever you want!" and by doing so
performed the god-like function of breathing
grit into me. Even my own sisters
were more concerned with hairdryers and boys
than with the poems I recited ad nauseum

in our shared bedrooms when the lights were out.
"You're making me sick!" my sisters would say
as I ranted on, Whitman's "Song of Myself"
not the best lullaby, I now admit,
or Chaucer in Middle English which caused
many a nightmare fight. "Mami!" they'd called,
"She's doing it again!" Slap of slippers
in the hall, door clicks, and lights snapped on.
"Why can't you be considerate for once?"
"I am," I pleaded, "these are sounds, sweet airs

that give delight and——" "Keep it to yourself!"
my mother said, which more than anything
anyone in my childhood advised
turned me to this paper solitude
where I both keep things secret and broadcast
my heart for all the world to read. And so,
through many drafts, I became the woman
I kept to myself as I lay awake
in that dark bedroom with the lonesome sound
of their soft breathing as my sisters slept.

VAIN DOUBTS

Years ago now—a breezy, bygone day,
walking a city street, my hair tossing,
feeling the beauty of my young body,
that animal friskiness triggered by spring,
I glanced admiringly at my reflection
in a storefront window, tossing my head
to watch that mirrored waving of a mane
I thought my best feature—when a young man
coming in my direction barred my way.
With great disgust, he uttered, "Vanity!"

And I was stopped in my mindless moment
of physical joy, shamed to associate
that deadly sin with the upsurge of life
and self-love I'd been feeling, never doubting
my urban prophet had been right. Vanity—
so this was what that ugly sin felt like!
In his disgust, I heard the click of keys
in convents, harems, attics, marriages,
down the generations, doors closing on
bodies that could give both pleasure and life.

Now that the years have granted me release
from such vain doubts, I'd like to post myself
at slumber parties, bathrooms, dressing rooms,
wherever young girls gather, frowning at
their wrong-size figures, blah hair, blemished skin—
already taught to find fault or disguise
joy in their bodies. I'd like to be the voice
that drowns out their self-doubt, singing in praise
of what I couldn't see when I was young:
we're simply beautiful, just as we are.

FIRST MUSE

When I heard the famous poet pronounce
"One can only write poems in the tongue
in which one first said *Mother*," I was stunned.
Lately arrived in English, I slipped down
into my seat and fought back tears, thinking
of all those notebooks filled with bogus poems
I'd have to burn, thinking maybe there was
a little loophole, maybe just maybe
Mami had sung me lullabies she'd learned
from wives stationed at the embassy,

thinking maybe she'd left the radio on
beside my crib tuned to the BBC
or Voice of America, maybe her friend
from boarding school had sent a talking doll
who spoke in English? Maybe I could be
the one exception to this writing rule?
For months I suffered from bad writer's-block,
which I envisioned, not as a blank page,
but as a literary border guard
turning me back to Spanish on each line.

I gave up writing, watched lots of TV,
and you know how it happens that advice
comes from unlikely quarters? *She* came on,
sassy, olive-skinned, hula-hooping her hips,
a basket of bananas on her head,
her lilting accent so full of feeling
it seemed the way the heart would speak English
if it could speak. I touched the screen and sang
my own heart out with my new muse, *I am
Chiquita Banana and I'm here to say . . .*

LUNCH HOUR, 1971

It was the autumn of my discontent
in New York City. I was twenty-one
with nothing to show but a resumé
of thin successes: sundry summer jobs,
a college-writing prize, four published poems
in a small journal edited by friends.
I got a job on 42nd Street
with *Special Reports, Incorporated,*
a series of newsletters that went out
to schools and libraries on hot topics.

I was put in charge of *Special Reports:*
Ecology and the new *Women's Issues,*
which I manned from the tiny broom closet
called my office, from which I could see—
once the leaves fell—two lions reclining
before the public library. That fall
our bestseller, *Special Reports: The World,*
was full of news about the Vietnam war.
The blood-red oak leaves falling in the park
outside my window seemed sad mementos

of mounting casualties a world away,
and closer in the choices I had made.
Each day at noon, I'd race down to the street,
past protestors handing out peace buttons
and stale leaflets I'd pretend to read.
I ate a quick snack sitting on the steps
between the lions, wiped my greasy hands
on their stony manes, and still hungry,
I spent my lunch hour in the library,
feeding the poet starving inside me.

HEARTLAND

Those heartsick days living in the heartland.
Those hard days that I thought would never end.
Houses so homey they seemed appliquéd
on the landscape, hedges and trees in place
as if they had been rented for each lawn
along with picket fences, pastel mums,
and politically incorrect lawn ornaments:
Mexicans sleeping with sombreros on,
black footmen with their faces painted white
out of some vague respect for civil rights.

My landlady had a lady on our lawn,
bent over so her frilly panties showed.
I'd look out at her and my heart would sink.
Depression is always in the details.
Homesick and lovesick, I kept mental lists
of objects that seemed sentient with advice:
churches like thumbtacks stuck in every block
to hold down what might otherwise rise up,
drapes drawn at dusk, tunafish casseroles
no one back east was making anymore—

back east . . . where the man I was obsessed with
was living on the verge of his divorce
——or so he wrote in passionate letters
utterly discredited in this setting.
Is this true love? I kept asking myself.
Desperate for answers, I applied to her:
What would you do to bypass this impasse?
But she just mooned me (with her panties on)
as if to say, *My dear, don't be an ass.*
Honestly, what a tiresome question!

BAD-WEATHER FRIENDS

Old friends from my other, less successful lives
who put up with me, how grateful I am
to each of you for how you saved the day
when all my days were dark nights of the soul.
I must have been one of those sad cases
you see on late-night movies, thirty-plus,
insomniac, twice divorced, unsettled, poor,
while the writing I used as my excuse
for my unhappiness was utter trash.
In short, not a pretty picture to watch.

And you, whose names I sometimes can't recall,
came out of nowhere with buckets and vans
to help me move to the next rental,
packing my books, my clothes, my manuscripts,
storing my overspill in your garages.
Some of you even let me stay with you
on living-room couches, fold-away cots,
telling me that old story: happiness
is around the next corner, heroines
were once sad women who got lucky.

You were right! At long last, happiness arrived—
a steady job, true love, a first novel.
By then, you, my bad-weather friends, were gone,
like thoughtful fairies in a Shakespeare play
who having cleaned up after our mistakes
tactfully vanish before the last act.
Now in my own house sitting at my desk,
looking out on a sunny autumn day,
I hear a roll call in the wind of thanks,
Zohreh, Jay, Greg, Judy, Marcela, Ann . . .

SISTERHOODS

I dream my sisters all gang up on me:
they hold a secret meeting and decide
to throw me out of the family, a vote
they're quick to point out is unanimous,
stripping me of my rank of sisterhood
for faults I'd rather not list—the gist being
that I am undeserving (which is true),
selfish, stinting, inclined to blurt things out,
which now compels me to defend myself,
using a phrase I read in a story

that goes something like this: we are saved
not because we are worthy but because
we are loved, and not just automatically
by God, who has to love us, but by kin
who don't. And so, my sisters' rejection
is like Adam's expulsion, only worse,
as he was promised future redemption,
but what redeeming purpose can there be
when my own sisters disinherit me?
The night of my dream was not a good night.

I wanted to call my sisters and find out
if any such meeting had taken place
behind my back. But it was past the hour
when they would welcome phone calls. So I lay
in darkness wondering what becomes of us
when we're beyond the pale of human love?
How can we earn the love that can't be earned
or make someone respond the way we want?
And lying there, I heard their voices call
from deep reserves of love, *Have faith, sister!*

REUNION

We hardly get together anymore,
now that we're busy with our families.
So, when my oldest sister calls to ask
if she, her husband, son, and new puppy
can come and visit, I say, "Yes, of course!
— only you'll have to leave the puppy home,"
blaming my cats and husband for my no.
She bristles at her end when I say so,
who once took orders from her. The visit
goes downhill from there: she accusing me

of being anal, rigid, controlling:
her mean shrink-talk, which I point out to her.
Still, when my sister leaves I press my hand
on her window, and she presses her hand
from the inside, looking into my eyes,
as if we were about to part for life,
she to a foreign country where she'll learn
new words for the world that we once shared.
Years hence, perhaps a great-grandson returns
to see the place that meant the world to her.

Already in this life, we've strayed away
to husbands, puppies, the way she believes
guests should be treated vs. my theories.
"If you can call them *theories*," she retorts.
At night, I hear her remaking the bed
the way she likes it, the sides not tucked in.
And I recall how when we first arrived
in this country, she'd yank her blankets loose
and reach across the gulf between our beds
to hold hands on those nights I was afraid.

MY BOTTOM LINE

You are the bottom line, my love, the net
that catches me each time I take a leap
toward an absolute that isn't there
but appears dispersed in the relative:
warm supper waiting when I get in late,
my folded long johns on the laundry stack,
the covers on my side turned sweetly down
when finally I head upstairs from work
that couldn't wait till morning, the love note
tucked in my suitcase for my night away.

It says the obvious, the old clichés
I wouldn't want my friends to know we use
for love. And god forbid my enemies
should get hold of these endearments,
so banal, I would lose my readers' trust
if someone published them under my name.
But still as I write mine (with smiley face)
and slip it under the pillow on your side,
or when I read yours in a hotel room
I feel more moved than by a Rilke poem

or a Tolstoy novel or a Shakespeare play.
My love grows stronger with the tried and true
if it comes from you. More and more as we age
and the golden boys peer out of the magazines
with their sultry looks and their arched brows,
I'm so relieved I'm not an ingénue
searching for you at parties, singles bars.
I have you, waving when my plane gets in,
curling your body in the shape of mine,
my love, my number one, my bottom line.

LOVE PORTIONS

We're always fighting about household chores
but with this twist: we fight *to do* the work:
both wanting to fix dinner, mow the lawn,
haul the recycling boxes to the truck,
or wash the dishes when our guests depart.
I don't mean little spats, I mean real fights,
banged doors and harsh words over the soapsuds.
You did it last night! No fair, you shopped!
The feast spoils while we argue portions—
both so afraid of taking advantage.

But love should be unbalanced, a circus clown
carrying a tower of cups and saucers
who slips on a banana peel and lands
with every cup still full of hot coffee—
well, almost every cup. A field of seeds
pushing their green hopes through the frozen earth
to what might be spring or a springlike day
midwinter. Love ignores neat measures,
the waves leave ragged wet marks on the shore,
autumn lights one more fire in the maples.

Tonight, you say you're making our dinner
and won't let me so much as stir the sauce.
I march up to my study in a huff.
The oven buzzer sounds, the smells waft up
of something good I try hard to ignore
while I cook up my paper concoction.
Finally, you call me down to your chef d'oeuvre:
a three-course meal! I hand you mine, this poem.
Briefly, the scales balance between us:
food for the body, nurture for the soul.

FIGHTS

Our fights, they last for days, not the fighting
but that long aftermath when neither one
wants to go first over the muddy waters
of reconciliation, waters churned up
by fears and jealousies we can't control,
bad weathers of the soul that sweep through us
leaving us both like those grim survivors
of natural disasters on TV
recounting numbly over and over,
"I never thought . . . next thing I knew . . . "

All happy families, Leo Tolstoy wrote,
are alike, but each unhappy family
is unhappy in its own unhappy way.
I'd rather be like everybody else,
humdrum and glad, tending my happy lot,
than standing in an open field littered
with what was once our house, the newscaster
probing with tactless questions in the hopes
we'll break down with our own unique
unhappiness before the camera.

Days after, we're still feeling the effects,
lights aren't back yet, the road's impassable,
the world mined with betrayals left and right.
Meanwhile in the back rooms of the heart
we count by flickering gas-lamp what is left—
not much when put in piles of yours and mine.
Outside the rivers overflow their banks
and thunder through our lives so we can't hear,
for all our righteousness, the other's cry,
perhaps of reassurance, perhaps good-bye.

TONE

I hear my husband on the phone downstairs,
not the exact words just a certain tone
that's wafting upstairs—and right off I know,
he's talking to his mother by the way
his voice relaxes, spreads like soft butter
on fresh bread. When he's done, I hurry down
as if to get a taste of him still warm
with mother love. So different from the tone
of tightened purse strings when his ex-wife calls.
I stay upstairs, not wanting to be pulled in.

Or his daughters call, and his voice skips stones
across the pond of longing that wells up
after a week of not speaking with them.
From bed, I hear him sweet-talking the cat—
no words, just the same coaxing murmuring
he's humming in my ear when we make love.
Me and the cats! I could be doing worse.
Or the clipped tone he uses to cut off
a telemarketer at supper time;
or a request to fund a dubious cause;

or the military yes-sir, no-sir tone
with which he passes information on
to people he dislikes; finally, the oh
so charming tone he dotes on my mother,
as if he has to prove himself worthy
to marry me. But we're already wed,
flesh and bone, so all I have to hear
is the vibration of his voice downstairs
and instantly I know what he's feeling
as if I felt that same feeling myself.

HAIRBANDS

My husband has given away my hairbands
in my dream to the young women he works with,
my black velvet, my mauve, my patent leather one,
the olive band with the magenta rose
whose paper petals crumple in the drawer,
the flowered crepe, the felt with a rickrack
of vines, the twined mock-tortoise shells.
He says I do not need them, I've cut my hair,
so it no longer falls in my eyes when I read,
or when we are making love and I bend over him.

But no, I tell him, you do not understand,
I want my hairbands even if I don't need them.
These are the trophies of my maidenhood,
the satin dress with buttons down the back,
the scented box with the scalloped photographs.
This is my wild-haired girlhood dazzled with stories
of love, the romantic heroine with the pale, operatic face
who throws herself on the train tracks of men's arms.
These are the chastened girl-selves I gave up
to become the woman who could be married to you.

But every once in a while, I pull them out
of my dresser drawer and touch them to my cheek,
worn velvet and faded silk, *mi tesoro, mi juventud*—
which my husband has passed on to the young women
who hold for him the promise of who I was.
And in my dream I weep real tears that wake me up
to my husband sleeping beside me that deep sleep
that makes me tremble thinking of what is coming.
And I slip out of bed to check they are still mine,
my crumpled rose, my mauve, my black hairbands.

MANHOLES

I love to see men coming out of holes:
manholes and sewer drains and train tunnels,
or down the poles of firehouses, the gong
going like crazy, a dozen heroes
in the making. Through the bedroom window
comes the housepainter to touch up my sills,
a college boy, naked from the waist up,
who talks of Nietzsche between drying coats;
or hauled up from my well the dowser calls,
"There's water!" as he dabs his sweaty face.

I'm known to gawk at men in coveralls,
jackhammering themselves into the earth,
then rising out of rubble like the dead.
Or the bell-ringing priest, pulling the ropes,
then descending through the steeple trapdoor,
one of God's discard angels without wings.
Perhaps it's their fragility I love:
that moment when they're caught in no-man's land,
plummeting through the dark, then coming back,
smiling, unscathed, with their hardhats still on,

no time to think of conquest, empires, women,
the makes of cars, the best in mutual funds,
who won the Super Bowl. No, they're knee deep
or more in circumstance: The mainline broke!
There's trouble in the bowels of the earth
that needs urgent fixing! When they emerge,
shaken by what they've seen, tears in their eyes
at disasters and deaths averted—that's when
I love them most—when they remind me of
that moment when their mothers gave them life.

CANONS

Preparing for the Pico Duarte climb
with only one-half of a packing mule
allotted to personal belongings,
I had to choose between Bishop and Frost.
Frost would be perfect for the dialogue
I planned to have with nature, but Bishop
was addressing a similar landscape
in her Brazil poems. I weighed back and forth,
considering leaving a second pair
of hiking shoes or my long underwear.

Finally——I hate to say it——but I chose
solely in terms of weight: the paperback
Frost was lighter, smaller than Bishop,
and would fit in my jacket pocket if
the mule got tired and had to be relieved.
This choice led me to think of how canons
are formed, how books are chosen as the texts
to be carried down the generations.
Why Pound and not H.D.? And why, oh why,
Sir So-and-So and not more Sor Juana?

I'd like to think the basis for the choice
was on some better principle than mine,
but who knows? Especially when I peruse
my old Norton anthologies and note
the shameful absence of certain voices,
I wonder if they never existed
or if they were knocked out of the running
for some silliness like the writer's sex?
Perhaps those who selected were like me
who let an ass choose my mountain canon.

MY KIND OF WOMAN

First off, we can start with Eve, who misbehaved,
taking a bite of the forbidden fruit,
a woman not afraid to risk God's ire
or Adam's blame to know good from evil.
Or Lot's wife—does she even have a name?
who suffered death because she chose to turn.
Oh, so to love the sight of what she loves—
the red roof on her house, her line of wash—
that she gave up salvation for a glimpse.
My kind of woman: bold and curious.

I like the quiet, pensive ones as well:
Mary, so often praised for the wrong things:
her humbleness, her sweet docility,
her loving parenting of Jesus Christ,
instead of her most worthy quality:
her Buddhist calm in the face of shocking news—
that she was pregnant with the son of God!
She didn't balk or ask to be excused
or worry what her parents were going to think.
My kind of virgin, guilt- and fancy-free!

Speaking of virgins, I'll end with Joan of Arc.
How many smart young women wouldn't want
to cut their hair and bind their breasts and roam
far from their fathers' houses on their own,
making the world safer for womankind?
I see a theme: smart ladies with big mouths,
on whom nothing is lost, big-hearted gals.
Husbands, priests, daddies, bosses, sultans, dons,
choose for your chattel the pliant, docile ones.
My kind of women aren't the ones you want.

MUSEO DEL HOMBRE

Santo Domingo, Dominican Republic

In the museo, the Taino queen,
Anacaona, has my sister's eyes.
And Duarte in the portrait where he's barred
from his beloved patria wears the scowl
my father wore in exile. Sánchez's nose
is replicated on my tía's face;
her sugar-cane skin matches Salomé's.
Mella is pouting with my mother's mouth.
How heartening and unsettling to see
history wearing the face of family.

Not only heroes, poets, Indian queens,
but tyrants, swindlers, conquistadors
could be close kin, along with their victims.
The master whipping the black servant girl
could be my cousin cursing his chauffeur
or Tía losing patience with her maid—
the same arched brows, the fury in the eyes.
These ghostly resemblances remind me
that our Dominican familia's not exempt
from all the highs and lows of history.

In museums, I always felt left out
of history with its pale northern face.
The pink-skinned Washington at Valley Forge
or white-wigged Jefferson were not my kin.
Even their blue-eyed wives, their blond children,
their little dogs seemed alien to me.
But now my people hang upon these walls
and history is pressing in on me,
as if to say, *¡Tu tiempo ya llegó!*
Become the one you have been waiting for.

ARS POLITICA

I was the daughter who changed overnight
from clingy, thumb in her mouth, a problem child,
always afraid and needing to be soothed
to feisty, elbows-out, watch-out-for-her!
What happened—so the family story goes—
was that I picked up reading and began
to make things up, to take the hurricane
out of the wind, bring back the disappeared,
replace the shanty shacks with palaces,
and turn the beggars loose on my vegetables.

I yearned to write the story of my life
into a book a girl might want to read,
a girl like me, no longer frightened by
the whisperings of terrified adults,
the cries of uncles being rounded up,
the sirens of the death squads racing by
toward a destination I could change
with an eraser or a trick ending.
There had to be a way to make the world
safer, so I could bear to live in it!

This might not be the destiny of art,
to save the uncles, free the prisoners
with a twist of plot, but it's a start
if Wordsworth had it right, and the child is
father of the man—but just a start.
The inhumanity of our humanity
will not be fixed by metaphor alone.
The plot will fail, the tortured will divulge
our names, our human story end, unless
our art can right what happens in the world.

NAMING THE ANIMALS

Let's name the animals no longer with us,
except in language: start with the dodo,
the Haitian long-tongued bat, the dwarf emu,
the laughing owl, the eastern buffalo.
And then animals like the nukupuu,
the lorikeet, the broad-faced potoroo,
whose absences don't sadden me as much
as I can't put a picture to their names:
two potoroos, say, lounging in their den
with baby potoroos clambering over them.

I think of Adam watching the parade
of just-created animals, their form
still taking shape, so had he touched too hard,
the camel might have had some extra humps,
the colors might have smudged on the peacock,
which wasn't yet a peacock, but a thing,
a brightly colored, gorgeous, feathered thing
in need of a name—as was the camel,
the marmoset, the deer, the parakeet,
waiting to enter language and be claimed.

But now, we, Adam's babies, find ourselves
uttering names no one comes up to claim:
no iridescent, billed, web-footed
quacks back when we say *Leguat's Gelinote*——
in fact, unless we say the name out loud
or write it down, the gelinote is gone.
And so, our language, which singles us out
from dwarf emus, nukupuus, potoroos,
becomes an elegy, as with each loss
our humanness begins to vanish, too.

THE ANIMALS REVIEW PICTURES
OF A VANISHED RACE

"Look at this most curious specimen!"
the cricket chirps, holding a photograph
of a line of chorus girls in bathing suits
kicking their legs. "I think it's more than one,"
the centipede points out. "But yes, they're odd."
"Wait till you see the markings on this one!"
the bulldog growls, tossing a black-and-white
of a chain gang digging in their prison stripes.
"No kin to us!" the outraged zebra shouts.
"Observe the evil flatness of their snouts."

Foxes, flies, penguins, ladybugs, lions—
in short, the whole animal kingdom has come
to celebrate the lucky extinction
of Earth's worst enemy and take a vote
on whether to elect a new top dog.
"Cease from using species-specific terms!"
the snakes protest. Of course, they're sensitive,
maligned for generations as the cause
of mankind's fall. Meanwhile, as next of kin,
the chimps keep bringing up the missing link.

After a *No!* vote, the animals pile up
the memorabilia of the vanished race—
pictures of kings, ice-skaters, terrorists—
then light the pyre. Not a trace remains
of those who poisoned, ravaged, exploited,
and robbed their common home—or almost none.
A love-struck chimp has sneaked a picture out,
torn from the frontispiece of a book of poems,
and hidden inside a banana peel,
of (possibly?) Emily Dickinson.

WHY DON'T WE EVER SEE
JESUS LAUGHING?

Why don't we ever see Jesus laughing
or cracking a joke or telling a tall tale
that makes his glum disciples hold their sides?
Seldom are they shown smiling. If at all,
it's Judas with the twisted mouth, that's how
in famous paintings you can pick him out.
But Jesus — do we ever see him break
into delighted chuckles the first time
he works a miracle and wine pours out
from water pots, saving the wedding day?

Nobody ever laughs in the Bible
except for the pregnant Sarah's belly laugh
or Yahweh's Ha! of the know-it-all in Job.
Probably God smiled on the seventh day,
looking down at creation, calling it good.
Let's hope. But it's His son I want to see
in stitches, infused with the holy spirit
of the ridiculous, a god made flesh
and full of nonsense, guffawing at the thought
that he is briefly dust and knows he's dust,

but also immortal! Maybe he smiled
at virgins toweling his feet with their hair
or fumbling Pharisees, but I want much more!
If I were doubting Thomas I would ask
to hear him laugh. Who cares about his wounds!
Loaves and fishes multiplying like rabbits!
Lepers with creamy skin! The lame leaping!
The blind seeing! Lazarus rising up
as if death were a nap! Good news galore!
I might believe him if he smiled more.

ADDISON'S VISION

Addison tells of spending his summer
clearing the farm his family has owned
since the revolutionary war,
acres and acres of overgrown fields—
pastures and hayfields, hedgerows, timberlands—
a big enterprise for an ex–farm boy
turned pastor in a flowing cassock
not handy for plowing. I've seen him lift
the bread and wine in pale hands above
the bowing heads of his parishioners.

Now as he celebrates the Eucharist,
I see the chalice turn into an ax,
the handle darkened with his father's sweat,
and before that, his grandfather's, on down
the generations until the sad phrase
delivered in the garden comes to mind:
sweat of your brow, which now is Addison's,
clearing the land so that we see the light
as it first shone on Adam, pruning turned
into a kind of hands-on ministry.

What did he see once the hedgerows were cleared?
The skies opening, divine light beaming down
on distant vistas of a promised land?
Salvation for God's sweating minister?
No, he saw only what was there to see—
rolling green hills such as a child might draw,
cars moving on a distant road like beads
on an abacus, a neighbor hanging wash:
the earth released and grown so luminous
that he was saved simply by seeing it.

WINTER STORM

It's snowing hard in the Green Mountains,
I haven't seen Mount Abe all morning,
just the white blur of an expanding storm
in the distance, while closer by, the town
is a pincushion of flickering lights
prickling through the haze. Hard to believe
the blowing snow is not the fallout from
this deepening depression that descends
and deadens everything. It's snowing hard
in the pasture below, the sheep are lost

in the commotion of the fleecy air,
so that it takes a leap of more than faith
to trust that they're still pasturing there.
My husband left in a whirlwind of snow,
as if his car were being whisked away
into some other world, leaving me here
to shovel out the silence on my own.
It's snowing hard in slanted lines across
the drifting driveway, muted fields,
in no time I'll be snowbound, no way out

to the small town where friends might take me in
and reassure me I've had a bad dream
I'm free to wake up from. It's snowing hard
for days now in the thicket of my heart
in which no ram appears to stop my hand
from plunging doubt's knives into what I love
as the snows come down and all my Isaacs die,
every last one of them from lack of faith,
and it keeps snowing until nothing's left
except the emptiness of the blank page.

THE THERAPIST

He seems tired. (I'm his last appointment.)
Being wise all day probably takes its toll,
having to know but not appear to know
so patients search out answers on their own.
"Right?" I ask him. He shrugs, "If you say so."
"On the other hand," he's fond of saying;
"You tell me what it means," he grins slyly—
transparent strategies, hoops I'll leap through
into happiness, if that's what it takes.
"Ah, happiness," he sighs, again the grin.

Weekly, we meet. The clinic waiting room
is strewn with cheap toys and old magazines
I never heard of: *Working Mother, Self,*
and one for kids with guessing games and jokes
none of them reads. One little girl tells me
her older brother's sick, "and mean," she adds.
Her frazzled mother scolds her, "Shut your mouth!"
lifting a threatening hand. "Sick!" she repeats
and bursts into giggles, and so do I.
I sober instantly when he appears.

We walk the endless hall. Along the way
the whirring noise machines outside each door
obscure confessions going on inside:
mothers who scold and swat, fathers who drink,
uncles who fondle, lovers who betray—
the whole sad gamut of inhumanity
we practice on each other, which is why
we've come here, sick and mean, to heal ourselves.
"Right?" I ask him. He's not supposed to say
what he knows, if he knows, what we're doing.

DISAPPEARING

I have slenderized. I have gotten thin,
thin as a wafer, as a piece of string,
a filling, a poor man's wedding ring.
Undressed of any excess, I blend in,
a blind stitch hidden in the tapestry
of the generations, a reluctant egg
shunning the lavish spray of eager sperm.
Why be a nine-months bother in the womb,
pumped with a bellyful of pretty hopes,
only to be born needy, colicky?

If I make myself small perhaps I'll fit
in the stingiest fist, the heart that never has
enough to give, the bully who wants it all,
the glutton who piles his plate to avoid the sight
of needy eyes that await what crumbs might fall.
After the feast there's bound to be a crust
on the master's plate, a meal I much prefer
to one that requires a toll of gratitude.
Better not compromise the seed of self
to whatever power wields the watering can.

And so I hug my body to myself,
pull in my nets, fold and refold my flesh.
What will be left for death if I succeed?
Only a trail of print on a page as clean
as the dinner plate of a goody-goody child.
After the feast of summer comes the fall
with its empty cup. Why mourn the shriveled leaves?
Less and less to belabor or become.
A nibble, a sip, a swallow—and I'm done.
I am disappearing. I am almost gone.

GAINING MY SELF BACK

Muscle on muscle, fat layered on fat:
arms, belly, buttocks, hips, thighs, legs bulge out—
I'm packing the body for return to life!
This is no resurrection from the dead,
but an escape from the anorexic hold
of losses that can't be helped, but pile up
like roadblocks at the borders of the self.
Each bite scanned, each calorie turned back
as if vigilance over each spoonful could ward off
the bitter taste of an old unhappiness.

I'm getting free! I'm going home! I dream
of piling my plate with seconds, drinking deep
from the cup of whatever's put in front of me;
filling my life to the brim and above the brim
with all that I ever wanted but never got:
a downpour, not a drizzle; a bonfire,
not a flickering flame. Bring on the feast,
the miracle of multiplying loaves
to feed a multitude of orphan needs
starved by the iron will of discipline.

Wherever I walk, footprints mark the ground.
Branches I brush by rustle. Birdsong stops
at my approach. I'm a human presence now.
Gone are my waif days, waiting in the wings,
my butterfly touch, my pretty satin things,
the beauty of the body vanishing . . .
No more withholding. I am almost home.
Deep in my self, a light has been left on—
as if somebody, knowing I'd return,
has set the table, kept my supper warm.

THAT MOMENT

when astronauts disappear behind the moon
and all contact with them is lost
until they reappear again; or when
firemen enter the burning building
and flames leap out of the hole they entered;
or during wartime as the train pulls out
of the station, a desperate hand waves
from the window, a voice calls out a name,
a voice the named one never hears again,
or when your child merges with a crowd—

those everlasting separations from
the people you love, the places you love,
to which you were intending to return.
But the moment passes; the train arrives;
you enter a new country, fall in love,
marry, and build a house with postcard views
of snow-capped mountains, babbling brooks—
clichés you never knew would feel so good.
But as you look out savoring the scene,
a chain of other mountains rises up,

a ghostly face composes in the clouds,
a loss you never thought you would survive,
but here you are far stronger, more at home
and happier than you ever were before.
Those hard moments that take your breath away,
and literally will do so at the end,
pile up like casualties and treasures, both.
Hold on tight! could be the first commandment
for this life, and the second, *Let it go!*
Only the empty hand is free to hold.

SIGNS

My friend said what was hardest were the signs
her mother left behind: a favorite dress
misbuttoned on a hanger; library books
covered in paper bags, way overdue;
a flowered cup she'd broken and glued back
crookedly, so the petals didn't match.
Her mother came to visit every year
and mined the house with madeleines that broke
my friend's heart every time she pulled open
a cabinet her mother had straightened.

Another friend said he waited for months
that turned to years after his father died
for a sign promised from the afterworld.
My friend said he would set up little traps:
if the light turns green . . . if the doorbell rings . . .
if the leaf falls before the count of five. . . .
Meanwhile his favorite maple shed its leaves,
replaced them, lost a branch in a windstorm,
burned gold—seasonal incarnations galore,
which my friend missed waiting for his dad's sign.

These stories came when I was full of grief
about my own losses, wondering what,
if anything, my words could do for those
broken on the hard edge of the world.
Vanity, I thought, this is vanity.
Roll up your sleeves and do something useful!
But here on paper, I fit piece to piece
until the roses match, the cracks are sealed,
the cup fills to the brim, and over the brim.
Drink, my sad friends, be briefly whole again.

DEATHDAYS

It used to be we marked time with birthdays:
huge childhood parties with wedding-size cakes
to celebrate that season's crop of cousins,
all of us dressed in costumes from countries
my grandparents had recently visited:
Mexican sombreros and toreador pants,
embroidered peasant blouses for the girls,
Dutch clogs and dirndled dresses with white caps,
silk saris, togas, grass skirts, Chinese thongs,
as if to meet the future in disguise.

But now it's death that singles out a date.
May 30th, my grandfather set out,
nine years after my grandmother who died
September 5th—I like to think of them
as on another one of their long trips.
A conscientious colleague died June 3rd,
right after turning in her final grades.
May 24th, March 4th—the dates are piling up.
My dressy black dress never gathers dust
with old silk saris, linen caps, Dutch clogs.

And then the other anniversaries
of near misses: a childhood friend wears
a padded top that gives no hint at all
of what is gone now going on five years.
Our church's mascot maneuvers so well
with her prosthetic leg her mom can quip
not even a crazed bullet slows her down.
And every year a day as yet unknown
which I won't be here to enjoy goes by,
which is why now I celebrate each one.

ALL'S CLEAR

The blaster at the building site next door
comes by with the stamped permit: *three whistles,*
blast within five minutes; two whistles, within
two minutes; and finally my favorite,
one whistle, all's clear. "Have a good day, ma'am,"
he says, departing. They call us *ma'am,*
these young boys with construction-worker tans,
whose daddies used to whistle compliments
at our young counterparts, before the ground
shifted, and our eternal youth came tumbling down.

The doctor checks the freckled skin and says,
nothing to fret about. He makes a map
of all my markings, a constellation
not in the sign of Cancer, but to be watched.
In the waiting room sits a box of knitted hats.
The sign reads, *Help yourself.* (I pick out one
for you, my balding friend.) The little tags,
handwritten by survivors, give their name
and last day of treatment—that sweet *all's clear,*
a red light turning green, spring's daffodils!

The first of every month, my husband checks
now one, now another breast, his eyes blank,
as slowly he palpates the soft tissue.
I hold my breath in dread of your surprise.
Thank you, I always tell him when he's done,
as if he'd stood on line all day to get
my permit stamped, *All's clear, for now.* —Meanwhile,
I wait for next door's blasting to be done,
the ground to still, the sky to clear of dust,
for you to call—*All's clear for both of us.*

NOW, WHEN I LOOK AT WOMEN

Now, when I look at women, I wonder
if a breast is missing, if a scar marks
the place like a pirate's X on a map
where a lump lay buried. I look at their hair
cut close to the skull and I wonder if
the style was chosen for its trendiness
or if it signifies recovery,
first shoots after a long, hard winter;
wildflowers in the woods; dandelions
on the lawn; a birdfeeder full of birds.

Looking at women now, I also see
the ones who didn't make it, tías, friends,
their faces surfacing in grocery stores
and drive-in windows, moms and bank tellers
whose carts I want to push, whose hands I take
as they tender deposit slips, at a loss
what to say: *I'm so glad you're here to spend*
a moment of this autumn day with me—
while they eye me, wary, wondering
what social service agency to call.

Suddenly every girl seems vulnerable:
their female bodies specifically marked
with little black spots like the mortal sins
in my old catechism book, the fear of death
palpable as I turned the page and read
about absolution through the sacrament
of confession. But only the surgeon's knife
and radiating beam might save these lives.
Even so, I can't help this helpless love
for every woman's child, daughter or son.

AT THE GYN

Seen from the parking lot, the building seems
an army barracks, every window lit,
with now and then a shape in uniform
casting a shadow as she passes by.
I'm glad it's not one of those offices
on Main Street that pretends to be a house—
as if your pap smear's one more household task
between the vacuuming and dinner prep.
I don't want the false comfort of a home
these days when news is likely to be grim.

Open the door, a few women look up
and smile, as if relieved to see it's me.
The waiting room's in total disarray,
toys from the toy box kids never put back
when moms were ushered in for their exams;
end tables strewn with pamphlets dull with facts,
and oh-too-many women's magazines
(most of them missing pages of coupons).
The bathroom's stocked with napkins, just in case;
the seat is down—somebody thought of us!

Barracks aside, this is a female stop:
the mess, the changing table, the request
you pay your bills on time, a tactful sign
framed with a smiley face: *Have a nice day!*
Everyone here except a stray husband
or pacing boyfriend awaiting the results
is one of us—as if the world in which
we come to know our bodies should be kept
a place apart where we can catch our breath,
surrender to our lives and to our deaths.

GRAND BABY

My husband says, why don't you write a poem
about the new baby, you're the writer
in the family, birth is a big deal,
it deserves a poem, "new life," etc.
Put in about her being born in spring,
on International Women's Day—
now there's a theme. I bet most poets write
about their kids and grandkids when they're born.
You're always scribbling about the past,
how about a here-and-now grandbaby?

Tall order but short notice, honey. I hate
to tell you but babies don't need poetry.
We do, we, intelligent people,
gaga over the crib, which thankfully
has a guardrail to keep people like us
from crawling inside to recite something
appropriate & unnecessary. Silence
is the compliment here—stunned and abashed
and joyous silence, a quiet reply
to the noisy mysteries of the universe.

Hello, Naomi, how you doing, girl?
is the best I can do when I stare down
at her tiny, elegant hands and dream
a pen, a little baton, a steering wheel
in them, trying to match a future life
with her astonishing & perfect self.
But I've taken her silence as my cue.
Naomi doesn't need a word from me.
I'm just a writer in the family.
I know real poetry when I see it.

LIFE LINES

Words I read years ago keep coming back
to calm me at the most opportune times.
Helping my parents pack for their return
back to their homeland after forty years,
my sadness lifted, murmuring a line
from Yeats, *That is no country for old men.*
When my niece told me she was marrying
a young man I wish I thought better of,
I almost said—but bit my tongue in time—
When lovely woman stoops to folly.

As Mom lay dying and I saw the light
receding from her eyes, the phrase popped up,
Creeps in this petty pace from day to day,
and I felt comforted as if my grief
could be contained within that mournful line,
and yet I mourned the deeper for that line.
Often I crack and poetry seals the crack,
I've glued many a heartbreak with the phrase,
After so many deaths, I live and write!
which sets me up to love and lose again!

Unlike my Buddhist friends I've never found
solace in silence. Sorry, but I love
the way words say what can't be said in words.
We fall and a brief quatrain breaks our fall.
A villanelle recalls us to ourselves.
I'm buoyed by poems that spring upon my lips
like prayers mothers whisper over cribs.
The winds of time would carry me away
but for the words which when my life breaks down
rise up and clap their hands and louder sing!

SPRING, AT LAST!

This is the first spring that I've noticed spring.
Incredible, I know, to miss so much.
Why did it take so long? Mom and Dad's deaths,
a friend's cancer, a cousin's accident,
the Twin Towers, the war on innocents
(always the ones to pay)—the End seemed near.
Then, suddenly, a daffodil, a patch
of crocuses, bird fights at the feeder,
and back into the intact Towers flew
stick figures, like a film put in reverse.

Each morning I wake up and run outdoors
to check the stingy inching of the grass.
I holler for my husband to come see.
"You're going to be the death of me!" he warns.
"I thought a hungry bear was after you.
Calm down. It's annual. It's only spring."
But like a star's light, beamed eons ago,
spring reached me just this year. I'm taking note
of peepers, pink skies, swatters back in use,
goldfinches, fiddleheads, forget-me-nots—

as if life really works in sad reverse:
when young, my youth got in the way——
my frizzy hair, my breasts not big enough,
my grand career that never seemed to start,
my many lovers who never appeared.
But now, amazing grace, I see, I see!
My life is giving me a second chance
as I take time to savor it at last.
All that I wasted, overlooked, bypassed
springs back whichever way I look, or write.

REGRESO

Late in his life, Papi forgets himself
and switches from his broken English
to his *muy eloquente español.*
My husband glances up at me,
flashing his monolingual SOS,
What's he saying? Or talking on the phone
about his imminent *regreso* home
after four decades living in New York,
he starts to roll his r's and sails off
into a stream of Spanish consciousness.

The family wonders if he should be checked,
if he's regressing, if he's showing signs
of early Alzheimer's, as he rattles on
about his imminent return, *¡Por fin!*
mi regreso a mi tierra. Ya yo estoy
cansado de traducción.—But I feel glad
that he is speaking in his native tongue,
after so many years of struggling
to bring all of himself into *inglés,*
and tell the great adventure of his life.

Now, he gives up midsentence, pours his sense
into the deeper cistern of his soul,
his native tongue — *¡La lengua mas bella!*
so he would tell me when in shame I'd beg
that he speak English with my teenage friends,
or rather (but I didn't dare say this)
that he keep quiet to avoid their scorn.
Now, as your final *regreso* draws close,
cuéntanos, Papi, todo en español,
all that we lost of you in English.

IN SPANISH

Sometimes it touches me more when I hear
a phrase in Spanish rather than English.
We're walking in the campo and a friend
warns me to steer clear of that thorny bush,
Esa mata hay que respetarla.
(That plant is one you have to respect.)
My old niñera answers my compliment
that she is looking younger every year,
Los años no perdonan a nadie.
(The years don't forgive anyone, doña!)

She calls me *doña* who once ran my world—
proof of her point that time topples us all,
but her saying it in Spanish goes deeper
and stirs the sediment at the bottom
of my heart, so the feeling is stronger,
more mixed in with everything else I am,
swirling through both the thick and thin of me,
leaving nothing unfeeling which is why
I've been accused of overreacting
when I change countries and forget myself.

It's puzzling then that I write in English,
as if I have to step back from myself
to be able to say what I'm feeling—
the way sometimes we have to get away
from the place we were born or from someone
we love in order to know who we are.
Yet as I write in English I murmur
the words over in Spanish to be sure
I'm writing down the truth of what I feel.
(Que escribo lo que siento de verdad.)

YOU

I love how English has a single *you,*
no *tú, usted,* no trying to figure out
where strangers rank in the hierarchy
of my respect: Are you a formal
or familiar *you?* No asking permission
or apologizing if I get it wrong.
I love the true democracy of *you.*
The pampered son of the dot-com millionaire
or the coal miner's daughter—all are *you,*
united in one no-nonsense pronoun.

Comforting when I write because it means
I'm leaving no one out, even a line
intended for an intimate includes
you, and also you. In this, my Noah's ark,
everyone is invited and can board
in twos or threes or singly—those unborn
as well as ghostly *antepasados*
who used to be *usted* and now are dust.
At sea in mystery, we all become
human cargo down the generations.

Once you get used to *you,* all faces seem
to hold the face you love, each child could be
the one you never had, each girl the girl
you used to be or who your mother was.
You is inclusive like that Beetle ad
where linebackers kept piling into a car—
I forget what the point was, but I'd watch
and understand their yearning to be one.
Just as I once climbed into a second tongue
and it made room for me in its pronoun.

LEAVING ENGLISH

Before leaving English, I cling to words
I haven't paid attention to in years:
dirndl and *trill* and *sin,* until the thought
of spending weeks without them is too sad
to think about. *Come with me,* I invite
my monolingual husband, so at night
you can whisper sweet nothings in my ears
against possession by my native tongue.
Even if Spanish made me who I was,
it's English now that tells who I am.

You talk like an addict, my husband scolds.
Language is not a drug! (But I get high
working a line until I get it right,
like finding the last puzzle piece or bulb
that lights up the whole string of Christmas lights!)
My family claims that I've deserted them:
One thing is learning English, another
to think you're lost without it, por favor!
You left in exile — that was not your fault.
This passion is a second desertion.

Before leaving, I touch the shelves of books,
then close my study door reluctantly
like a child casting a longing glance
at bedtime at her bears and dressed-up dolls,
posed to enact some simple ritual,
a tea party, a classroom scene. *Stay!*
Don't you dare move! But English won't obey,
no living language will. When I come back
it will take *días* to collect myself,
pieces of me not fitting anywhere.

MEDITATION

Sometimes I'll walk out in a field at night
and sit under the stars, breathing in stars,
moon, sky-reflecting pond; breathing out stars,
moon, sky-reflecting—*Whoa! What was that?*
A beaver in the pond? And now, a flood
of other thoughts rush in—*my aching back;*
so and so's email; oh god, I forgot
to pick up garlic! Soon, I cannot hear
the owls hooting, the leaves rustling back,
carried away by today's trivia.

Sometimes a busy, brassy place seems best:
a shopping mall Saturday afternoon,
crowded with warring teenage girls and moms,
and little boys out of some matinee
practicing their Karate kicks and cries—
all of that roiling, noisy humanity
I carry deep within me which is why
I need to meditate. But sales beckon,
shoppers hurry by, the food court fills, and down
the spiritual tubes goes my meditation.

My final stop is always on these lines,
a breathless shipwreck crawling up a beach
that seems deserted, not a sign of life.
But in this emptiness, I find myself
and lose myself as lines move in and out
like breathing, like discovering a space
which by turns is a shopping mall, a field,
a pond, and all and none of the above.
It's hard to call what happens here a name—
my poem, my practice, my meditation?

AFICIONADOS

I have a friend who tangos and attends
meetings in Helsinki, amazingly
the largest convention of tango lovers
in the world: day after chilly day
the couples one-two, swoon, one-two, and turn,
across the mirrored ballroom as snows fall
beyond the steamed-up windows. Just last year,
he met a dental hygienist from Maine
and fell madly in love. I see him dancing
in shiny black shoes and red cummerbund,

she in a long (I think, required) skirt,
a slit revealing vistas never seen
in Maine, vistas she surely never sees
peering down throats, her hand on countless cheeks.
Another man I know adores *Star Trek*
and meets with other Trekkies once a year.
Get him started and the dinner party
is ruined, except for the amusement
of seeing him so worked up. Every month
I send a dying stamp-collecting friend

stamps saved from letters sent by island aunts,
gaudy virgins, miniature dictators,
flowers so otherworldly my friend says
he'll soon be seeing native specimens.
The man who cuts my hair spends his spare time
making doll furniture. Each time I hear
of some new passion, I feel gratitude
at one more instance of the many ways
we learn through what we love to love the world—
which might be all that we are here to do.

TOUCHING BOTTOM

Sometimes the best advice comes randomly.
"Please hold through the silence," the machine voice said,
the best advice I've ever come across
for weathering writer's block. At the restaurant,
my friend tasted her buffalo steak and said,
"It's not like anything they say it is,"
which words should be engraved upon my heart
and piped into my memory each time
that I assume the saying of the world
is anything at all like living in it.

And yet, I love how words can sound the world,
how they can take you deep inside your life:
you say something simple, and suddenly,
that plank in reason breaks and down you drop—
into a liberating train of thought.
You're drinking coffee, talking to a friend,
and poetry unravels from *her* mouth,
an Ariadne string that leads you out
of that dark labyrinth where a minotaur
of your own making has held you in thrall.

"Keep your end level," my husband advised
as we built shelves, and as the high-strung one,
I took his words to heart. "Take in my give,"
my mother used to say as we made beds,
which words taught me how to conduct myself
in future bedrooms with the men I loved.
My self-made father once said, "We should live
like poor men with money." When I thanked him,
he asked, "For what?" I said, "Because I just
touched bottom in my life when you said that."

CLEANING LADIES

I feel so strange when she's cleaning my house
while I'm writing away in my study.
I'm half-tempted to join her on all fours
scrubbing the tiles, waxing the hardwood floors.
Not only that but she's an older blonde
(older than me, I mean) and also trim
like a movie star. Back where I came from,
ladies like her have maids who look like me.
How odd to have the tables turned on us —
tables which she has polished, I might add.

I try to ignore her and do my job —
working her language — while she writes me notes,
misspelled and overpunctuated
with exclamation marks: *Bathroom lite's broke!!!*
Need more Murphy's Oil & Mister Clean!!!
Whatever she asks for I indulge her brands.
Once when the local paper did a piece
on my writing, she asked about my books.
I gave her a signed copy of each one.
She never said a word about them.

She probably thinks I'm wasting my time,
writing, rewriting, filling the garbage bin.
(She's emptied it and seen the dozen drafts.)
One of these days, I'm going to ask her in
and show her that I'm also working hard,
polishing verbs, sweeping out excess words,
mopping up sticky adjectives, adverbs,
hoping to make her feel as much at home
in her own language as she makes me feel
in rooms that rhyme and sparkle with her skill.

TOM

stands before his triptych—three self-portraits—
in the photo I took and later titled
Portrait of the Artist as a Creation
of His Creation, or more playfully,
What Came First, the Real or Painted Tom?
The first two panels show the painted Tom
struggling to lift himself from the backdrop,
as if to free his body from his work,
but sinking back down in the last panel
into the careful brushstrokes of a fire.

Seeing him through my lens, I wonder if
there's any way an artist can escape
his work and be simply himself, plain Tom?
Tom's pose seems to suggest it's possible
to be the young creator in control
of his creation—but behind his back
the triptych mocks him with a triple self
as if to say this making and remaking
is also who you are. It touches me,
this quadruple portrait of the young artist:

the triptych and then my picture of Tom
standing in front of the triptych
in black jeans, black shirt, a white undershirt—
as if all color went into the work,
and Tom's the washed-out version, what remains
when the feast is over, and the soul joys
in its temporal boundaries, which is why
I've hung this photo by my writing desk
as a reminder that we make our art
out of ourselves and what we make makes us.

I DREAM OF ALLEN GINSBERG

April 6, 1997

The night of Allen Ginsberg's death I dream
he comes to visit me, tearful because
one of the best poets of our times has died.
I embrace him, patting his heaving back
as if I were burping a big baby,
telling him how sorry I am, asking
if he'll recite some lines by the deceased.
"I saw the best minds of my generation
destroyed by madness—" He breaks down sobbing.
Allen, I say, that's yourself you're quoting!

"It's all the same," he says, and takes me up
on my invitation to spend the night.
He makes mi casa, su casa, all right!
blaring his old LPs, dropping acid
and dirty clothes wherever he takes them off.
Upstairs, I trip on a purple parasol,
which I assume is his. Meanwhile, downstairs
my island familia pulls out all the stops,
cooking sancocho, pastelitos, flan
for el muchacho who needs his strength to grieve.

Vexed by the relatives and added mess,
I stay upstairs, reading the day's headlines:
"Allen Ginsberg Dies"! It's up to me
to go tell him. Howling laughter drifts up
as he regales my tías with upbeat
tales of his naughtiness. I brace myself,
descend the stairs with newspaper in hand,
and slip behind his chair, tongue-tied, weeping.
Allen looks up, bewildered. "Jesus Christ!
It's raining in here! Where's my umbrella?"

FAMOUS POET, YEARS AFTERWARD

There he is on the podium, the famous poet
who pulled on my toes the night I stayed in his house
over twenty-five years ago—a young MFA-er
invited to crash on the couch by his beautiful wife.
Surely, he's joking, I told myself back then:
the man is old; he's already got a girl
for a second wife! Next time it was his hand
tapping my thigh as he read out my villanelle.
"I'm here for poetry," I protested. He laughed.
"So am I, darlin'! You've got to loosen these rhymes!"

This went on . . . I complained to his buddy
who ran the department. He paid me no mind,
complimenting my "talents," promising
to have a little talk with the old goat,
a nudge and a hand slap over bourbon and rocks.
By then, I had dropped out, feeling ashamed
as women often do when Eden, marriages,
or dreams don't work—a sin to have refused
to be muse fodder for a great man's work,
using the lame excuse: I'm here for art.

But then, a glorious revenge ensued:
he disappeared in anonymity!
Over the years, I never heard his name
in writerly discussions, never found his books
whenever I searched the shelves, relieved each time
he wasn't there: another hammer blow
on the coffin lid of a ghost. —Now, here he is!
(no justice in the life or in the work?)
a grizzled éminence, pronouncing stuff
some girls in the front row are writing down.

WHY I TEACH

Instead of babies, I've raised my students,
hundreds of them, truly, thousands of them.
I've been an indiscriminate teacher:
September after September, I say, "More!"
Instead of their first milk tooth, baby steps,
I celebrate first sonnets, villanelles,
sestinas, slant rhymes, risky enjambments
when they push over the edge of a line
as if down a steep slide. "Hooray!" I say.
They haven't heard that since their playground days.

I've weathered their stormy rebellions, too,
the adolescence of their young talent,
when all they want to do is write free verse
—with emphasis on *free*—and only read
Adrienne Rich, Mark Doty, Sharon Olds
since everyone else is dead and white and male.
(But Mark *is* white *and* male, I note.)
Wisely, and while they rage, I read their poems,
sending them back for one more revision.
"Aren't you ever satisfied?" they complain.

They go off pouting to revise their poems.
"Hey, guys," I want to call out after them,
"This *is* the writing life! Get used to it!"
though I could just as well say, This is life—
the chance to try a new draft every day,
to work at what you love until the work
becomes a way of life you can't give up
but have to share with others on the page
and off the page—in subways, nursing homes,
novels, bedrooms, essays, classrooms, poems.

UNDERCOVER POET

Under the cover of novels, I write poems.
Between the first chapter where my heroine
meets her hero and the second where they fall
in love, I scribble a sonnet or I read a poem
by Billy Collins and fall in love again
with poetry. Why go to the trouble
of describing the house, the doctor, the malady,
when all I need is Emily's fly buzzing
in the sickroom or Blake's wildflower
to understand eternity in four lines?

Periodically, I ask myself why. Why
give up my quiet isle of Innisfree
to board a noisy ocean liner, filled
with characters in conflict, squabbling
with each other or themselves until
three hundred pages later they decide
to change their lives? Believe me, I believe
everyone needs a voyage, a week on deck
with all the messy, roiling humanity
a heart can take, but then come home to this.

In Catholic school, I'd tuck my *Leaves of Grass*
inside my opened catechism book—
How many persons in one God? I'd yawn
and end up poring through the lustier poems
omitted from our Whitman sampler. Did I
already understand that subterfuge
is part of poetry, that I have to tell the truth
but tell it slant? That on board, when asked
by a fellow passenger, "What do you do?"
I should answer, "I write, mostly novels."

SMALL PORTIONS

The earth is just too big, too beautiful:
I like it small, through a window, catching
the light at the day's end. I prefer poems
haiku-size; a pair of binoculars
through which I see one bluebird at a time,
the pink bib at its throat, the lacquered claws
curled upon an apple bough with the fruit
just setting on, a green miniscule globe
in whose meat I can taste Adam and Eve,
the whole sad history of our human grief.

See what I mean? Take one small thing in hand,
open it up, and there's another door,
and another, long corridors of views
into the heart of darkness or of light.
There's no such thing as a small portion
once you bite in and savor the flavors.
If truth is in the details, I'm the pope
of the particular, imam of mites,
a god in the minus numbers, a worm
pearling the soil with the teensy bits

I take in and deliver, laboring on
my two-inch by two-inch ivory life.
Friends worry I'm missing the big picture.
But I can hear a chorus in one voice,
and just this morning from my study chair
I watched a master bluebird build Versailles
in a maple's cubby hole. By the compost bin
I've got an ant hill of the pyramids.
My lot's to be a nibbler at life's feast.
Bit by bit, I'll devour all of it!

"POETRY MAKES NOTHING HAPPEN"?

Listening to a poem on the radio,
Mike Holmquist stayed awake on his drive home
from Laramie on Interstate 80,
tapping his hand to the beat of Longfellow;
while overcome by grief one lonesome night
when the house still held her husband's pills, May Quinn
took down a book by Yeats and fell asleep
reading, "When You Are Old," not the poet's best,
but still, poetry made nothing happen,
which was good, given what May had in mind.

Writing a paper on a Bishop poem,
Jenny Klein missed her ride but arrived home
to the cancer news in a better frame of mind,
The art of losing isn't hard to master. . . .
While troops dropped down into Afghanistan
in the living room, Naomi Gordon clapped
to the nursery rhyme her father had turned on,
All the king's horses and all the king's men. . . .
If only poetry had made nothing happen!
If only the president had listened to Auden!

Faith Chaney, Lulú Pérez, Sunghee Chen—
there's a list as long as an epic poem
of folks who'll swear a poem has never done
a thing for them . . . except . . . perhaps adjust
the sunset view one cloudy afternoon,
which made them see themselves or see the world
in a different light—degrees of change so small
only a poem registers them at all.
That's why they can be trusted, why poems
might save us from what happens in the world.

READING FOR PLEASURE

When I read a book I love, I fall in love
with the author, I can't help it, the voice
even if centuries old pierces my heart
as if along with every reader, I
were being threaded through a needle's eye
that's being used to stitch the lot of us
into an uncommon humanity
of lovers for whom books are love letters
posted to every man, woman, and child,
but penned specifically to each of us.

How many times haven't I stroked the sheets
of my Riverside Shakespeare, or pressed my lips
to my dog-eared Dickinson! I pine for Keats
whenever I read his odes, and I confess
I want to be Maud when I reread Yeats.
Each time, I teach George Herbert, I caress
the page on which my favorite poem appears
as if to soothe the weary minister
who asks, *Who'd have thought my shrivel'd hart
could have recovered greenesse?* I did, George!

Perhaps I picked up this desire from them
of wanting my readers to fall in love
with hairbands, willow trees, lawn ornaments:
this odd and wondrous world which would be lost
without our recreations—those who write,
but principally those who read for pleasure,
breathing life into dead characters.
And now, like them, I lie on these cold sheets,
waiting to be a woman once again.
You who are reading these words come closer.

DIRECT ADDRESS

I love those poems where writers turn to me,
addressing me as *you*—and though I know
that thousands upon thousands of readers
have trod his *Leaves of Grass,* I'm still convinced
it's me Whitman's instructing when he writes,
Look for me under your bootsoles.
The signs of those we love are everywhere,
their ghostly faces rushing by on trains
or forming in the clouds; nurseries belie
the stony closures in the graveyard.

That is the only way the dead come back
as far as I can tell. My grandfather
surfaces in the locust's gnarled trunk,
so comforting to touch his face again.
The bulldog wears my fourth grade teacher's scowl;
I back away as when I was a child.
Pachelbel's canon calms like Chucha's arms.
And what a shock to find in a Vuillard
my grandmother peering out as if to catch
the lazy maids at their shenanigans.

I'd like to think this is how I'll come back:
lines in a poem that spring upon your lips,
though who the author was has slipped your mind.
It's agency, not fame, I want: my words
at work, a slap awake, a soothing hand.
But since death's likely to transform my wish,
there's no direct address that I can give
where you should look for me. So you (yes, *you!*),
keep watch! I could be under your bootsoles
or inside this poem already inside you.

PASSING ON

Emily in one hand, Walt in the other,
that's how I learned my craft, struggling
to navigate my own way between them
and get to where I wanted to end up:
some place dead center in the human heart.
I've had an odyssey with both along:
Emily with her slant sense of directions;
and rowdy Walt, so loud and in my face,
I've had to stuff his mouth with leaves of grass
at times to hear my own song of myself!

Such mixtures are my forte after all,
Since I prefer the hyphenated voice,
a little of this, a little of that,
my tías gossiping while rolling dough,
my mother malapropping her clichés
(Don't try to judge a forest by its leaves),
Gladys intoning her sad boleros
as she sweeps out the house of childhood,
Milagros with her saucy salsa songs,
my godmother telling her rosary beads.

And most of these voices not in English,
some in Spanish, and some in that first tongue
when all I knew was heartbeat and the hum
of Mami's murmuring blood becoming mine.
And now this mix of voices sails out—
a Tower of Babel crammed in Noah's ark—
into the future silences beyond
where I can go and where those yet unborn
might read what's left of me, this voice
I now pass on, my own, and not my own.

Keeping Watch

EL SERENO

Nights of my childhood, he made his rounds,
the old sereno with his dim flashlight
whose batteries were always dying out.
I found out why: the maids would borrow them
to play their little radio all day long.
(How else keep up their spirits but with song?)
In their distraction, I would slip away
to the sereno's hut, waiting for him
to wake up midday, grim-eyed, sour-faced.
"What do you want?" He'd shoo me off to play.

Even back then, I was impressed by him:
his wise-man face; his narrowed, piercing eyes;
his lack of interest in frivolities—
untangling my kite string, baiting my line.
He was worn out with carrying the load
of all he'd seen during his dark patrols.
Some nights, he'd stop—I'd hold my breath
until his footsteps passed—*All's well. Dream on.*
Sereno was the name I knew him by.
Serene and *dew of night,* his homonyms.

A lifetime later, I'll wake up mid-night,
to utter silence—2 A.M.! That time
when our eternal, mortal loneliness;
the losses that await us or have come
steal like intruders into our sleepless minds.
"What do I want?" the ancient question lurks.
Serenity, to bear the heavy load
with grace. High spirits to inspire the heart
with song and not alarm the ones I love—
those dreamers who will soon be waking up.

LOOKING UP

Why is it we like looking at the sky?
In part, of course, we're checking weather:
masses of dark clouds or a stormy haze
or breakthrough blue can alter a day's plan.
But even after we've gotten the gist
of mist or drizzle, we keep looking up—
perhaps a habit copied from the Greeks
who used the heavens as a crystal ball,
foretelling future from the flights of birds
or leaves blown in the air and spinning down.

In the more recent past, astonomers
studying the stars predicted character.
And not counting the Moslems who look east,
and Buddhists whose third eye is looking in,
most other world religions aim their prayers
skyward where a Higher Power resides.
I'm no exception, I'm still suffering
from that residual spiritual tic
of looking upward for more certainty,
a dove descending, angels winging down.

But though I'm scavenging for the divine,
what holds my gaze are signs we put up there:
some child's runaway kite, a jet's brief glint,
light poles and traffic lights, the Goodyear Blimp—
the margins of our human drama where
we battle desperately for some control,
which we are bound to lose, the kite string snaps,
a patch of color sails into the blue,
beautiful in its insignificance.
We watch it as it dances out of view.

WHAT WE ASK FOR

The only thing that Jesus ever asked,
of a personal nature, was on the night
before he died: he asked three apostles,
James, John, and Peter, to stay up with him.
My soul is sorrowing to the point of death.
It was his humanness that needed them.
What else to ask for since he had to die?
Three times he asked, three times they fell asleep,
until sweet Jesus finally said, *Sleep on.*
It's done. My hour has already come.

The Sufi mystic Rumi urges us,
Do not go back to sleep. And Lord Krishna
rallies the sleepy Arjuna to arise
and join the fray of an awakened life.
Buddha has taught us to breathe in, breathe out,
in order to stay mindful, stay awake
watching our current incarnation roll:
¡Latina poet! Next time around, who knows?
It seems the great religions all agree
in what they ask of followers: *Stay up!*

As an insomniac, I understand
the loneliness of waking late at night,
wandering the house, checking on loved ones' sleep,
covering a child, filling a water glass.
Outside a cold rain falls. This night could be
the last of a doomed planet gone to sleep.
My soul is sorrowing because I know
that staying up won't save a blessed thing.
But oh, sweet Jesus! given what must come,
what else to ask or give our companions?

WHAT WAS IT THAT I WANTED?

What was it that I wanted? I forget—
to have a place called home, these quiet hills
I look on as I write, the trees I grew
as seedlings now full-blown and full of birds,
sparrows and thrushes singing as I work;
even the snow beating against the panes—
I wanted that. And you, dear one, stopping
outside my study door, then going on . . .
that loving pause that longs but still respects
my solitude—I wanted you most of all!

I wanted a voice, oh yes, one that would tell
simply but with the mute heart's eloquence
who I was, what my brief time on earth
was all about. And more, there was always more:
I wanted to be wanted, to belong
in school, country, gender, neighborhood—
one of the good girls everybody loves,
the heroine of the story of my life
with a happy ending. I wanted that—
who knows why anymore?—but yes, I did.

Some things I wanted but I couldn't get
I wanted not to want—my mother's love,
that look of urgent cherishing I've glimpsed
in the soft eyes of dogs and the dying.
I wanted Papi's love unhinged from shame,
his own and mine. I wanted not to feel
that yearning for the child I never had.
What else was it I wanted? I forget.
Or could it be the longing that I want
To make me stretch beyond the lot I got?

KEEPING WATCH

Watching the baby, I think of the dying,
of their grimaces, of how they throw their arms
or kick their legs, struggling to free themselves
from some invisible entanglement.
I think of my concentration on each breath
they're laboring to take, pacing my own
to theirs as if to help with the hard work
of staying alive. I stand by, hoping
to hear their voice saying my name
one last time——as if I were watching the baby,

listening for the slightest sound of sense:
a doubled syllable; a wail that means
Pick me up! I'm bored; or outraged scream,
I want my mother now! I want my milk!
Watching the dying, I'm struck by the same look
as in the baby's eyes, taking me in
without a judgment in the world as if
they're simply curious as to who I am,
a naked look which I return, *Oh yes,*
I see you, too. We are here together.

Watching them both, I think about myself,
how similar I feel, same helplessness,
same tenderness, same forgiveness for all
that's over and to come, all eyes, all ears.
I hold the freckled or the spotless hand
to feel its living warmth against my warmth,
to smell the smells, putrid or sweet,
that either way spell life. And doing so,
I realize that it's me who comes alive,
watching those coming in, those going out.

WHY I WRITE

Unless I write things down I never know
what I think, no less feel, about the world.
I found out first in print that I prefer
white wine to red, the blues to rock,
the winter's terseness to the spring's green gab—
conclusions reached in short stories or poems.
Once I, a vegetarian, tried red meat
because a recently divorced woman
on a blind date (in a poem I was writing)
ordered a well-done steak which turned out raw

and bled when she cut into it, a taste
I had to taste in order to describe it.
I'm not kidding: unless I write things down,
I don't know what I want: long lists of pros
and cons on a bedside pad, love letters
(How else can I be certain I'm in love?),
thank you's for gifts I never thought I'd use
until I jotted down my gratitude,
rhetorical addresses to a God
who only answers when I write Him down.

As far as I'm concerned the world's a blur
which each word in a sentence focuses,
as if I were fine-tuning the lenses
on my binoculars from bird to thrush
to Bicknell's thrush singing in the maple
for lack of pen and paper this spring day.
In short I don't know I'm alive unless
I'm writing as I'll only be convinced
—when I am scribbled on some stony epitaph—
that I am gone . . . and the rest is silence.

DID I REDEEM MYSELF?

Did I redeem myself, Mami? Papi?
Was I the native child you dreamed up
as you lay in the foreign bed you'd made
your first and failed exile in New York?
Did I excuse your later desertion,
leaving your friends behind to die? Did I
help to reframe that choice as sacrifice:
you gave your girls the lives they would have missed
growing up in a double tyranny
of patriarchy and dictatorship?

Did I redeem myself, my sisters, for those nights
I kept you up with Chaucer lullabies?
My love poems at *your* weddings? My calls
at midnight with a broken heart? And you,
dear lovers whom I mistook for husbands,
do you forgive me for forsaking you?
I heard—or thought I heard—a stronger call.
This love did prove the truest, after all.
And friends, can this be tender for your care?
Have I kept some of my promises here?

But harder still, my two Americas.
Quisqueya, did I pay my debt to you,
drained by dictatorship and poverty
of so much talent? Did I get their ear,
telling your stories in the sultan's court
until they wept our tears? And you, Oh Beautiful,
whose tongue wooed me to service, have I proved
my passion would persist beyond my youth?
Finally, my readers what will you decide
when all that's left of me will be these lines?

Notes

The series "Seven Trees" is for Sara Eichner and Berit Gordon.

"Abbot Academy" is for Ruth Stevenson as well as for
   Jean St. Pierre, two dear teachers who *trained* me at Abbot.

"Grand Baby" is for Naomi Stella Gordon.

"Addison's Vision" is for Addison Hall.

"Signs" is for Anamie Curlin.

"All's Clear" is for Susan Bergholz.

"Tom" is for Tom Krueger.

"'Poetry makes nothing happen'?" is for Jay Parini.
   The title is a quote from W. H. Auden's poem
   "In Memory of W. B. Yeats." The question mark is mine.

"Looking Up" is for Sara Eichner, inspired by her skyscapes.

"Keeping Watch" is for Mom and Dad.

Some of these poems have been previously published:

"Seven Trees" was first published as a limited edition book
   (North Andover: Kat Ran Press, 1998).

"By Accident," in *A Poem of Her Own: Voices of American Women
   Yesterday and Today* (New York: Harry N. Abrams, 2003).

"Bellevue" and "The Therapist," in *Bellevue Literary
   Review* 2.2 (Fall 2002).

"All-American Girl," in *Beauty's Nothing*
   (New York: Arena Editions, 2001).

"Manholes" and "Why Don't We Ever See Jesus Laughing?"
    in *Green Mountains Review: Comedy in Contemporary American
    Poetry*, 15.1–2 (Fall 2002).

"Ars Politica," in *Dream Me Home Safely* (Boston: Houghton Mifflin
    Company, 2003)

"Addison's Vision," in *Contemporary Poetry of New England*
    (Hanover: University Press of New England, 2002).

"All's Clear" and "Now When I Look at Women," in *mamm*
    (July–August 2003).

" 'Poetry makes nothing happen'?" in *Cry Out: Poets Protest the War*
    (New York: George Braziller, 2003).

"Regreso," in *Latina Magazine* (June 2003).

Thanks and Gracias:

To my readers, Judy Yarnall, Bobbie Bristol, Elisabeth Scharlatt,
    Susan Bergholz, Bill Eichner.

Siempre, Virgencita de Altagracia.